Focus on Life

Focus on Life

Mr. Jagmohan Singh

Foreword

This book has been primarily written for young people who are starting off in life. I wish I had received this knowledge when I was a teenager. Most of the points may seem like common sense, but they should help to pave the way ahead.

I hope that this book will assist students in learning to work hard and to reap the benefits in becoming successful. The only way forward is to be organised, planning work and leisure days with a diary and budgeting money carefully. This book is a guide to help you start good money habits, in motivating yourself to work hard and to be able to divide your earnings appropriately before spending on the all-important things in life.

Finally, we discuss building strong relationships with our network of family and friends. They too will help us to reach our goals throughout life.

I hope you find this useful and that it provides inspiration for your future success!

Jagmohan

Contents

CHAPTER 1

I started as a salesman

Yes, that's right. I started as a salesman in the 1990s.

I began my working life as a part-time salesman in Tottenham Court Road. At the time my boss had few shops. In his day, business was hard. We sold TVs, video players, hi-fis and headphones, etc. We were only earning a small commission.

Making a sale in those days was hard. How to sell became very important. My boss held a small training session after work and so we had to stay behind after hours for another half an hour or so. Quite a few years later mobile phones arrived from the top technical firms such as Motorola, Samsung, Nokia, etc. They were large multinational names. Companies like us, at the time, were selling phones for about £500.

Because of the demand, I decided to become an independent mobile phone salesman and I received a lot more commission in the heydays. However, Motorola continued to sell the 8500 and 8800 phones and the popular accessories made big profits for them.

After this we experienced the popularity – if you were lucky – of home cinema with Bose speakers, etc. Selling these became all-important. It was crucial to get to know your product well by researching its use and, therefore, making sales became far easier. Finding ways to close deals quick before the customer changed his or her mind was both a skill and a challenge.

Instead of diving into the deep end with the customer, you need to make them feel important by asking them questions; what are they looking for, what do they want to use it for and how much do they wish to spend? Of course, some customers already know the answers to these questions, but some do not!

The key fact is that, if a customer says they would like to spend £300 or more you need to upsell, which is when a seller invites the customer to purchase more expensive items, upgrades or other add-ons to generate more revenue. In 1990, selling was still hard but face to face sales were good.

There are a couple of things I remember – waking up at 7:00 to leave the house at 8:00. I would start work at 9:00 – like a robot for six days a week. On Sundays I would visit my local temple for prayers. I would then play football at 4:00. In those days there were no computers or mobile phones for entertainment.

Life continued like this for about ten years before I realised I wanted to make changes to my life. I decided I wanted to own my life properly. In my mind, I wanted to become my own boss. I knew it would be difficult because I would need the money to start up my own business. I began to research what I could do to achieve this.

In 1990, I started selling at Saturday markets in Finchley Road, Hampstead NW3. I sold phone accessories such as cases, aerials, holders, etc, with big profits. This was a massive opportunity for me to learn how to sell and do business. I learned even more about selling face to face to the general public – as you can imagine, I had to deal with all sorts of customers.

Also at this time there were films that were inspiring to me such as those starring Bruce Lee, James Bond and Rocky. By this stage, most people had more time on their hands, not like nowadays where you can buy everything online because everyone is too busy to visit the shops and retail parks.

Most people still had the old-style cars. I had a Ford Granada and my father owned a Volvo. Fixing your own car was quite normal in those days as it was cheaper and car engines were a lot simpler than they are now.

When I worked at the shop, all sales people were on commission and every month there were targets, which were hard to meet. Time is money because eight hours of the day you are working.

Looking for new work in retail was difficult

in the 1990s, however, I tried to focus on sales all the time because selling and how to do it properly is an important skill; after all, people need to buy things all the time. If a customer comes to your store asking for an item that you do not have, you need to upsell to change their mindset. For instance, if they come in asking for a particular TV, a 32" Sharp that you haven't got in stock, you can ask them, 'Why Sharp?' and 32" has a high price. You need to sell them an alternative, one that is better, cheaper or even bigger. For instance, you may have an LG TV 40" with a better picture, which also has a bigger screen *and* you have it in stock. You can provide them with the key features that are better. The customer can agree with you and hopefully you have a sale. Perhaps there is also a longer guarantee period on this alternative TV that you are about to sell to the customer – now the customer is on your side because you know your product. He came in for a Sharp but you sold him an LG because you knew your product. Your customer is happy, you're very satisfied with yourself and your boss is pleased as you've made a sale, *and* you've earned your commission! If you can keep up with professional sales skills like this then you will earn more commission each day, for sure.

You could also sell accessories to the customer to make more profit for yourself. This example can be given to any merchandise you wish to make a profit on, but to reiterate, knowing your product well is key, whether it's a car, clothes, a house or a boat. Remember to upsell if necessary.

Key points from this chapter:

- Focus on your job.

- Learn how to sell.

- Ask the customer what they want.

- Upsell, if necessary.

- Know your product.

- Knowing how to *sell* your product is just as important.

Notes

CHAPTER 2

Marriage, family and friends

In your 20s or 30s, or whatever age it may happen to you, getting married is a big part of your life. I got married in the 1980s when I was 25 years old. Finding the right partner who is loving and kind is wonderful. Someone to share your dreams in life and someone, with whom you can be yourself, is great for the soul.

Do not make the mistake I made where you may think you're too old to start again – you're not. No matter what age you are, you can still get up and start again in life.

If you wish to, starting a family could be a further step towards fulfilling your life. The hand of God is always there for you, and your family should be the same. However hard starting a family can be, slowly but surely it will be okay through compromise, love, work on both sides and, with it, the joy of looking back on a happy 25-year marriage.

Each person's expectations and ideas of marriage can vary. There is give and take in the form of compromise on each side and it requires work. It is difficult to explain, but until you get married you will understand what I'm saying. I got married in 1987 and entertainment was different back then as people had more time on their hands and enjoyed visiting cinemas, restaurants and theatres, etc. We weren't quite so 'busy busy' with having to juggle everything in life that we do now. We had more leisure time to spend with family and friends. The American soap *Friends* had begun in the 1990s, which provided real inspiration in spending time with your own friends; for instance, people would entertain and have friends round for dinner. Try it yourself; it helps to seal a close bond.

I still know my English teacher whom I met in a bookshop after 25 years. He looked at me,

I looked at him but I recognised him as he was just the same. He said, 'Jagmohan, is it you?' He was very happy to see me again and asked me about my family and what it was I was doing. I told him briefly about my day-to-day life.

In life, having a good friend, a close mate, who is honest and kind and on your side at all times is very beneficial, whether this be a best friend, your wife or life partner – someone you can rely on and whom you can call in the middle of the night – they are there for you, morning and night.

Once you have those children it is much better if you are established in a job and have a strict home/work routine so you have a boundary between family time and work time. You need time and money to go out and buy clothes, toys and books, etc. I will come onto budgeting in another chapter.

Children are very hard work. When they're babies they cry at night and later on you need to try your best to bring them up correctly. This is where good family and friends come in to help. You have to take your children to school and make sure they are okay until they're about 18 years old.

Having a positive attitude is so much better than a negative one. Anything you do for them you must try and have a positive passion for and then hopefully your attitude will rub off on them.

I found that sitting at a round dining table brings the family closer together and allows for good conversation; however, times are a'changing but this is a really lovely thing to do – having a simple meal together and sharing in the joy of it. It has always been normal for me and I recommend it to anyone. Nowadays people have computers and DVDs to distract them, but in the 1970s no-one could come to the table with a phone – they didn't exist. If you have to watch your favourite programme while eating, at least discuss it together.

The times I spent on family holidays have been good memories of mine. They instill love and affection for your family if you're lucky enough to be able to go on holiday together.

My old school friend became a policeman

and I bumped into him in a shopping centre after 20 years. Now we go for coffee together.

Friends can be a good 'contract' for your work or social life, as well as being good contacts!

Whether families are big or small, the principles remain the same… With running a household there are items you own such as a mortgage, a car and perhaps a business, etc. All these things require money to pay the bills.

Money and children

Children need to be trained in the way you work, so bring them up with a good work ethic; this can be reading books, homework, jobs around the house or cleaning the car, etc. Earning pocket money early is a good idea. From the outset, a child should be shown how to respect money from around their fifth or sixth birthday. They should also be shown examples of how to spend wisely and work hard at their studies. It is a good idea for children to start part-time jobs from the age of about 15 to understand the value of money. My friend says his grandkid is always asking him for money. I said to him that his or her parents should encourage them to do small jobs around the house to earn pocket money.

So, for me, after being married for 33 years, I find that love, happiness and friendship is key. Being honest, loving and honorable are also great assets to hold in life.

My family comprises my wife, four sons and one daughter. We come from India. My father came over in 1949. Back then it was hard to find work as well as bring up a family.

Discipline is important and will take you a long way in life. This is why *how* you bring up your kids is important – they relate to routine and behaviour thresholds through life and will hopefully experience the same lovely standard of living when they're older, just as they did when they were younger, and so on through the generations. Be loving and kind to your family.

At the moment I am writing in the midst of a pandemic and so currently our pubs, restaurants and shops are closed, making home life a little harder, however. We also have a lockdown in place, we need to wear masks and stay two metres away from other people.

With a family life, everything revolves around money, so the sooner you start saving money you will have something for a rainy day. Love is free though! If you need more money, family and friends can help which is why it's such a good idea to stay in contact with them and build a happy relationship – homeless people are homeless because they haven't got these relationships.

If you are thinking of setting up a new business, advise your friends and family – they will be full of knowledge and knowledge is power. If you are undecided on anything then they will help you with your decisions.

People say God is bigger than all. Have faith in God and you will do well.

Key points from this chapter:

- Be loving and kind.

- Focus on family and friends.

- Work hard to keep your marriage together.

- Look after and bring up your children well.

- Teach children and grandchildren the value of money.

- Work hard to pay for the family things in life.

- Make happy memories.

CHAPTER 3

Working six days a week

When I started my job in 1989 I worked six days a week, 9:00 to 6:00. I woke up at 7:00 am and came home at 7:00 pm. For ten years I was like a robot working away for someone else and not realising at that time that I could fulfill a dream of having my *own* business. I was not thinking about the future or an easier way to make money such as purchasing something for £10 and selling it for £20.

In the end I got bored with my job. My next term of employment lasted two years. After that I got tired again and began a new job, this time for three years. In total, I worked for 15 years for someone else. The penny started to drop and I began my own business. I started building work on a self-employed basis, but it was hard at the time. After this I became a lettings and sales negotiator in the property market. I had to find buyers and tenants. In around the year 2000, the estate agent business was big. This was when I bought my first property with a mortgage. After some time I also got interested in shares and building that part of the company

When I was a teenager I never used to read but when I read my first book about Lord Alan Sugar in the 1990s, I gained much business knowledge and understood the way forward. This book is called *The Amstrad Story* by David Thomas (1990). Another was called *Rich Dad, Poor Dad* by Robert T Kiyosaki. It made some very good points about life and it was this book that inspired me. Another great author that I recommend is Dale Carnegie, an American writer and lecturer who developed courses in self-improvement, salesmanship and other skills. He has written a couple of books, one of which is *How to Win Friends and Influence*

People (1936), which sold 16 million copies – so it's well worth looking him up. One person who read this book was Warren Buffett. It changed his life for good, so if you purchase this book I recommend you keep it for further reference. Knowledge is power. 'The more you learn, the more you earn' was a saying back in the day. Your wisdom of learning will never end if you keep on reading.

Make notes while reading notable points – stick them on your desk or noticeboard to remember them. Study the books and look up words you don't understand. If you read just one page of a book each day it could make you read 365 pages in a year. If you have fingers in many pies you can make money in seven ways. So, wealth *can* come fast.

At work, the people around you become family over time. Every day you spend hours working with your colleagues. Where I work in a retail shop, we once had 12 staff. Each one had a different side of interest but it is good because you can learn from them. Try and enjoy your work life as we spend many hours there.

Be organised for waking up in the mornings for work. I recommend waking up at 5:00, two hours before starting work and then you will see the difference it can make to your work life and success.

I was dealing with customers who had BMWs, Mercedes and Ferrari cars that would inspire me to own cars like that one day. I remember daydreaming about it at the time. My kids could ask, 'What will you buy us this Sunday?' and I could say, 'Toy cars or a Gameboy,' which, at the time, were popular.

In Hampstead, people were rich with big homes and cars, etc. There was a famous pub called Jack Straw's Castle, which my mates and I would go to each Friday. We would go in from work and have tea or coffee.

My work routine was that I'd start at 9:00, have my break at 10:30 for 15 minutes, lunch from 1:00 to 1:45 and then a 4:00 tea break until 4:15. I'd finish at 6:00.

I would recommend you never open a letter in the evening. Why? Because if the letter is a bank bill or summons, you may not sleep well.

It is best to deal with it in the morning when you have slept well and your head is clear. When you open that letter in the early morning you will think about your response in advance of writing back or making a call at break time.

There is another saying, 'Word hard and play harder'. Saturdays were hard days for me. Workdays were hard, but I learnt a lot. Some of the tasks I had were to take money from customers, pull the shutters down, clean the shop and to make sure everything was tidy at the close of day.

Life is about thinking sharp in order to be able to get up at 5:00 every day if your job demands it. Make it a habit. Go to bed at a sensible time. This will help to ensure you rise in time for work. Get yourself organised the night before and allow enough time for travelling. This will also help your mental health if you are caught up in any delays. You can do so much if you control time. Time is money. If you plan your time you will win every game you play in life.

I remember selling a mobile phone case to a customer. The case was black but she wanted a brown one and we didn't have it in stock. She came back after two weeks and we changed it for her. She was so happy because it matched her handbag. My message is – keep the customer happy at all times. There is another saying, 'The customer is always right'!

Helping to make customers feel satisfied with their purchase and acquiring more sales is wonderful. Keep up with the customer's desires and always try to persuade them to buy more.

We had an electronic Caseo till which was new at the time, but all staff were happy to operate it even though they were hard to use.

I liked working in retail shops, face to face with customers. I loved meeting people to learn from them and I gained much experience.

My teacher said 'It's not where you start but where you finish that matters most'.

Work hard, play harder and you will be successful. Teach your kids this as soon as possible. Teach them to read books, study hard and write. Keep them well; help them get successful in life.

Key points from this chapter:

- Wake up early.

- Try to start your own business.

- Live your dream and fulfill your goals in your work life.

- Make customers happy.

- Try to make friends with colleagues and socialise with them.

- Work hard and play harder.

CHAPTER 4

Things to do before and after work

What I learned over the years is planning ahead is paramount. Make the most of that one-hour before and after work. Plan your evenings so that they are not wasted. Being organised is a great habit to get into and something you should start sooner rather than later. It's a great habit to start – don't be lazy.

For instance, you need to have your dinner in the evening for an hour or so. Think what you could do for an hour before and after you've had your dinner.

Split your hour into four quarters, so every 15 minutes:

- Read from a book
- Sort clothes out for work tomorrow
- Empty bins
- Check your bills and letters.

Four different tasks; now if you do this five times a week you will have completed five hours of tasks and 20 jobs and will reap the benefits.

This is what I learned from one of my managers. He was around 60 years of age. I was 25 years old at the time and I was young, not appreciating at first what he was saying. If I listened to him properly I may have retired at 50 years of age, so planning is important and you must persist with it.

If you wake up at 5:00 am and you normally start work at 9:00 you have a 4-hour head start.

If it takes you one hour to get ready to get to work you will have three hours to play with. These three hours have to be planned. Plan whatever you are doing, whether that's a business plan, writing a book or housework. Tidy your clothes or fix things as soon as they get spoiled or broken; it is a good habit to get into. You could use the hour's extra time you have to do these things.

If you have 15 minutes for each task you have to achieve in a day, you can do 8 x 4 equals 32 tasks in a day. It's called FOCUS.

You will have more time on your hands if you are organised in life. Wash your clothes in the evening after dinner and let them dry overnight.

Many times we feel we do *not* have time, but you can learn to set aside the time and plan properly.

The average age for a normal, healthy human being to die is around 75–80. From the age of 1–28 you grow and learn. From 25–50 years you're working hard and from 50–75 you start slowing down. So, if you do 10–15 jobs whatever they are, you will become an expert in planning your time in order to get jobs done within a full-time working life.

Many people have a hobby before or after work. They may take the dog for a walk or perhaps they have a fish tank, rabbit or a cat to tend to. Some people go to the gym after work; others train at home or watch TV. It is important to build in that leisure time too.

Rather than save all the chores for the weekend you could clean the car at some point during the week and spend that weekend time for meeting friends or family (the good stuff!)

Always think time is important. Why? Time is money. Because making sure you're in the right place at the right time in your life is important and so is being positive. Don't take your time for granted.

I understand that this may not always be possible if you work late nights or do overtime, but the time off from work you *do* can be used positively.

As I mentioned earlier, if you wake up early, go for a jog and then take a shower, perhaps enjoy a tea or coffee afterwards – you will feel fresh and ready to go to work. Always plan to do something before you set off.

Planning your weekends is important because you have 48 hours to play with. You have worked hard during the week to earn your weekend time. Hopefully you will sleep well.

You don't want to work 32 hours at the end of your working week.

Some 'chores' may be hobbies for some people such as painting, cleaning the kitchen, bath, garden, etc. These jobs do need to be done at some point to enjoy a happy work/life balance. If you do not enjoy these things and haven't been able to factor in time during the week for them you will resent having to do them at the weekend – you will not have spent your time properly. There is always something to undertake but if you do *not* do a little each day it soon builds up, as well as the resentment. Arguments can take hold in your family time. Have a good work/life balance. Take more time for yourself too.

Sometimes I would open my door at the end of my working day and there'd be lots of post on my floor. As I said earlier, I would pick it up and leave it on my dinner table for the morning to open with my tea or coffee. Why? Most of the letters were bills… While driving to work I would think about which bill took priority to pay. If you do not do this, you risk going to bed worrying about paying the bills, which isn't great for sleeping.

You could clean the bins at night so in the morning they are done. These small house jobs can help. Cleaning the house at *all* times can bring you down if it is all you're spending your time on (unless your job is as a cleaner), and you don't want to spend the whole weekend doing it, so it's beneficial to be able to plan some time in during the week. It does work for some people – if they do the entire housework in one go it can bring them happiness and a sense of achievement that they have a clean living space for the rest of the week.

My mother said 'Always keep your kitchen clean because you never know who may come for coffee or tea'. Very true!

As soon as you have finished your dinner you can wipe down the table, clear away the dinner things and wash up so that you are not left with the mess in the morning – especially if you have woken late. If you do it straight away your kitchen is already clean and tidy in the morning and you're ready to make your breakfast and start your day in the right way.

Even keeping a 20ft x 20ft garden can be transformed just by spending 20 minutes a day on it – in six months it will look different. Do not spend more of your day making it look good, as time is important for other important stuff, unless of course it's that day's task

Making lunchtime food in the mornings for that day's lunch can certainly save you money. After you have finished your evening meal you could see what you have left over; perhaps it would make a handy sandwich or snack for tomorrow's lunch. One, it will be useful; two, it will save money rather than spending £3–4 at lunchtime.

My mother and father said 'Never waste food because you work hard for it by waking up and going to work every day'. Many people just eat fruit at lunchtimes to stay healthy, which is obviously good for everyone.

Key points from this chapter:

- Remember your parents' good time-keeping habits.

- Wake up at 5:00 am.

- Start good housekeeping habits.

- Plan what jobs you can do before and after work.

- Split each of those two hours into four parts for different jobs.

- Keep the bills for the morning.

- Spend a little time on tasks each day.

- Do not spend all the time on one task.

- Try and keep the nice jobs for the weekend.

CHAPTER 5

Upkeep of house

We touched a little on the last chapter about planning your time properly in order to be able to carry out chores during the week. In this one I focus more on the actual chores.

So when people say 'keeping up with the house' it means setting aside some time to focus on maintaining it, hopefully avoiding large repairs.

There are certain jobs that need doing every day, every other day or even once a week, for instance, cleaning the toilet, bath and showers, etc. Most mornings before leaving for work, I would empty the bins and take the rubbish out.

Painting and decorating jobs can be very rewarding if you 'do it yourself' because hiring these tradespeople can cost a lot of money. If you plan your time properly, you could set aside one whole day of the weekend to paint one or two coats, or perhaps you may finish the job and you will be pleased you have the other day free.

Refurbishing your property can take days. If you do it stage by stage and focus on one thing at a time then it prevents any panic over how much you need to do. You can finish the whole flat/house in a matter of days if you have the time set aside or you've booked time off work. For example, the first day of work you could do the ceiling of your living room, the second day, two walls and then the final day, the last two walls. The room is now finished and you have only spent about three–four days on it – saving time.

A few mornings a month I will look around the kitchen living areas to see if there is any damage. Building 15–20 minutes into your day here and there for checking and doing bits around the house is a great habit to get into and is very beneficial. Cleaning regularly for short periods is better than spending one whole day on a piece of work because you got behind with the cleaning; as I said, though, painting for one whole day on the time that you've set aside for yourself is cheaper than hiring a decorator.

Many households have drainage sinks that need to be kept clear as much as possible. All you need to do is get some salt, pour it into the sink or drain and then leave it for an hour and it will clean itself. Calling a plumber is costly; however, always have a good plumber's number handy in case something crops up that you're unable to handle yourself. Back in the days, every two weeks my dad would check the sink trap to see if it was clear of blockages. Calling a plumber would have been £40–50. Likewise with dripping taps –drops of water over time can become a sea.

There are many ways of saving money by 'doing it yourself' and nowadays of course you can watch YouTube videos for practically any house job that needs doing, and they will show you how it's done.

If you don't think you'll get the yard/garden

done this week then perhaps next week you could get a bit done before going to work? Or perhaps you could share the work with good friends and family, offer to cook them a meal in return and enjoy it in the garden.

Outside of lockdowns, life can be busy with weddings, birthdays and other social gatherings, so focus on the spare time that you *do* have. Always be aware of how to save money such as cleaning your windows, inside and out.

I had a friend who built a shed over two months, spending one hour after work on it. He designed and built it specifically for what he needed it for, which saved him money buying a costly one from a garden or home improvement centre.

Keeping your bedroom and clothes tidy at all times can not only help you feel organised but feel better about your space at the same time. Get into the habit of hanging your clothes up or taking them to the bin as soon as you take them off. Making your bed as soon as you are dressed in the morning is a good start to the day and is a good habit to help you keep tidy.

Make good use of spare storage space in your house/flat so it's easier to keep tidy at all times.

When you learn that you need to work hard for yourself, manage your money *and* your time properly, it is very rewarding when you are able to pay bills and fit in the housework too.

Some people go jogging or do weights, etc, then have shower and go to work. This makes for a great start to the day.

In the evenings, wash your dishes before you go to sleep so that when you wake up there are no dirty dishes to clean. Floors need to be mopped, carpets need to be hoovered. These jobs will hold until you wake up, but if you set aside a little time each evening then these things will already be done for you in the morning.

Keeping pets is sometimes hard when you are working, so make sure you have time for them. For instance, you will need to walk the dog before work and this will enable you to get your exercise and fresh air at the start of the day and you will have time to think about the rest of your day.

If you're stuck in traffic on the way to

work, use the time productively. It's a useful opportunity to catch up with the news on the radio or to plan how you're going to spend your time later.

Do you like cooking? Now, if you like to do a special meal on a Friday night for instance, you could wake up at 5:00 before work and have two hours' planning time. When you come back from work, a nice meal is ready for you in the evening (especially if you use a slow cooker). That's what I do and when you call friends round for dinner it's a great time saver.

This is one way of saving time – but always keep good time also. When starting a job, big or small, you are running against time.

Key points from this chapter:

- Set time aside each day to do small or large household tasks.

- Keep your bedroom and kitchen tidy.

- Check drains for blockages.

- Maintain kitchen worktops.

- Plan what jobs you can do before and after work.

- Try to carry out DIY where possible.

CHAPTER 6

Money problems

Money is a thing that is always a concern. Why? You need money all your life for one thing or another. This chapter concerns the process of saving and spending your money by setting budgets and getting into good habits.

Ensure you manage your money every month or you will be short. Why? Every month you will have new charges concerned with money.

My friend used to say 'A penny saved is a penny earned'. Once you have received your pay cheque, you will need to divide it up so you know how much you have to spend on that month's bills, lunches, insurance, direct debits, rent/mortgage, and hopefully, if you've been able to save anything, perhaps some money for going out or to put straight into the savings pot. For instance, you could divide it into three sections; 50% for bills, 30% for going out and 20% for saving every month. This will help avoid money problems.

Always pay your bills on time, otherwise there will be charges and you end up paying more in the long run, which just isn't worth it.

This habit will help you to save better for a rainy day when you have money problems. So think when buying, 'Do I need this item or can I live without it?'

Lots of people do not make a plan for money or budgets whatsoever. They are never able to save money.

Food shopping

- Make a list of everything you need so that you do not buy things you do not.
- Get pound coins instead of notes from the bank to make sure you do not overspend, but hopefully you will have coins from your saving jars (see next point).

Saving money/budgeting

- Scatter jars around the house to start saving money each day. As little as £1 will give you £30 at the end of the month. A small amount over time can become a large amount of money for a special purchase or to invest further.
- At the end of the month, if you put away £1 x 30 and times it by four it gives you £120 after four months, and after 12 months (a year), you have £1440.
- Encourage your children to start saving at an early age. Watching many motivation videos on YouTube can help you save money.

These plans may take time to implement, but it's getting into the habit of doing them. After three months it should be normal practice for you.

In researching this book, I have spoken to lots of business people and companies who tell me that the best way forward is to budget your money. Try to avoid owning credit cards but to pay for everything by debit. However, if you do a lot of on-line spending then credit cards are the safest option here, this is in case someone manages to steal your card details. If you are careful then your credit won't build up, giving you unwanted sleepless nights!

It is always advisable to pay your council tax via direct debit, setting this up in advance with your bank or building society, but if the money isn't there your bank will charge you leaving you in a worse position than you started. If money *is* there that's great and you have a much better frame of mind.

In the 1990s, most people would pay by cheque, but cheques are hardly in use nowadays unless you need to send money to someone in the post and you do not bank on-line.

You will never have money problems if you focus on saving money for different jars; one for council tax, two for gas and electricity bills, three for mobile phone and car or motorbike, etc. There is also car insurance and your phone bill to pay, etc, so always keep on top of things. There are always sundries that we need to pay for, those unexpected costs, so it's a good idea to have spare money.

Always try to get a good night's sleep to remove stress and refresh you for the next day. Try to think positive at all times. This will help you enormously in life.

Finding ways to save money for a better life is important. Can you find more ways than one to make money?

Still having problems?

- Perhaps you are unfortunate enough to have lost your job or are made redundant – it can be very hard without money.
- Try as hard as you can to find a weekend or evening job.
- If you're still experiencing problems, having done all of the above (other than being able to change your job to a higher paid one), you can do the following:
- For large purchases such as wedding rings, holidays or a car and you are lucky enough to receive a bonus or have saved a lot of

money, put £500 in one box, then increase it every month by £25.00, for 12 months.

- As mentioned earlier, get a jar and put in £1 every day for back-up. It will give you £365 after one year, and after three years you will have £1095.00. You must try and resist spending it at all times for this to work of course!

- What I have given you are only examples for you to work from; you can go higher or lower with these amounts.

Sell for cash:

- You can sell unwanted items on-line on sites such as Gumtree and eBay or even to friends.

- If you're crafty you could make items to sell in your spare time – perhaps you have a special talent?

Long-term investments:

- Plan ahead for further investments.
- Invest in high interest building society or bank savings accounts.

- Add to a competitive pension each month.

Long-term investments:

- Plan ahead for further investments.
- Invest in high interest building society or bank savings accounts.
- Add to a competitive pension each month.

People say money is hard to save. Yes, it can be, but if you focus every day you will get there. Stay focused on outgoings and budget accordingly. Money problems only come if you overspend your budgets. When the COVID-19 pandemic hit (and we are still enduring it now as I write in 2021), it has grown tougher than ever with businesses closing down and people losing their jobs.

Finding the money and saving is hard but if you can divide £10 in three different ways then you can save money. My teacher told me that if you are organised you can get to where you want to be faster.

Meeting deadlines is important, so try to pay

those bills as soon as you are paid. Don't get charged for late payments. Work your way to success brick by brick; do not look back. It may take you a decade of hard work to get there, but keep believing in yourself.

To achieve your goals in life you must spend wisely. Money can give you a bit of a confidence boost at these times.

You cannot buy love no matter how rich you become!

Key points from this chapter:

- Divide earnings up each month.

- Always pay bills on time.

- Make shopping lists – avoid overspending.

- Have money-saving jars around the house.

- Get a second job if necessary (part-time).

- Sell your unwanted items.

- Invest in long-term money-building plans.

CHAPTER 7

Becoming successful

Success comes with working hard day-by-day, brick by brick. Many people have reached their success brick by brick to get where they want to be.

A regular stream of income with a good job, an organised home life and some spare time means that you can make even more money if you have disposable income left over to use for this purpose, be that selling on-line, weekend employment or other things such as banking money in stocks and shares, etc.

If you follow the advice I have given you so far, after ten years or so of working hard you can reap the rewards and look back and see what you have gained. Remember that waking up at 5:00 or even 4:00 will make a difference to your life. Lots of people wake up at 4:00 when it is calm and peaceful. The brain is fresh to read for pleasure or plan the tasks of the day. Plan every hour of your day.

Planning and making budgets, at all times, will make a difference. It's not necessarily where you *start* in life but where you *finish* that matters. I worked for 18 hours a day and slept for the other six hours to make the difference. If you become successful you could be inspirational to others in need of help.

Learn from exciting business people by reading a book about them, for instance Warren Buffett, whom I mentioned earlier (there are at least 47 books in print with his name in the title). If you have the time while on holiday, why not read for 8–9 hours a day? You will gain valuable knowledge on their rise to success. You could also look at their company records.

Have mentors like Lord Alan Sugar, Jeff Bezos, Will Smith, Elon Musk, etc. They will show you the way to success. After all, if they can do it, why can't you? They all began somewhere.

Make progress by planning and looking at your goals. You will win eventually if you do this day to day. By making small progress each day you can tick the items off one by one.

As mentioned in the previous chapter, find products or services to sell or make and you could market your services to make money. Being your own boss is great, but if you have a 9–5 job you will always be a worker, not a businessman.

Many people do not plan daily, weekly or monthly, but you should plan each day like it is the most important day – focus on things you want to do to be successful. If you want to be a successful organiser you will be the winner in the long-term. Becoming successful takes time, it does not happen overnight. It needs hard work and so you must continue to FOCUS. If you do it bit by bit you will get there; success is found with patience and hard work and if you have many different strategies of making money then it should be made easier for you.

If you are very ambitious, start up a business and focus on building that business. Make sure your product is better than your competitors'.

I like to see people make money for themselves to bring a better life. Enjoy your family and friends. Being better off does not necessarily bring happiness but it can certainly help with all the bills, but some bills will pay for the good things in life – going on holiday and having a nice car, etc.

The power of money is good. When you are successful, look back and think where you started and where you have finished. It will bring you good feelings and confidence.

Failures will make you more successful. You will learn from your mistakes – lots of start-ups fail, but never give up hope. Always keep trying and one day you will get there.

Keep working hard; find ways to move forward even if you are saving just £5 a day, which, in one year's time will become £365. In five years it will give you £1825 for holidays, a birthday party or even a wedding cake.

But be *persistent* in your goal. It is important to make good habits every day and it'll take you places. Above is an example – you could save just £1 per day and it will give you £36,500 over three years and £109,500 per annum.

These are starting point habits and, bit by bit, they will help take you to a successful life. Never give up, always get up and start again; after all, it is FREE.

If you follow this advice and work hard, play harder, be organised and always budget in your 20s or 30s, then by 60 years of age you will hopefully be looking back on a successful career and be ready to retire (if not earlier!)

If you have planned to become more successful, find a new start-up business perhaps started by someone else, which you could invest money into – perhaps a friend will be following this venture if you do not do it yourself?

The product you're selling or purchasing must be competitive with the market. It could be a car, computer, clothes or food but must be cheaper and better than your competitors'.

When setting up a new business, research and re-research your target group and how best you can purchase materials, etc. It could be making cakes or selling computers. If you spend just ten minutes a day over 7–14 days it will help you to learn the market that you want to get involved with. A business that has discipline will go forward, not where you started. It can take 7–10 years for businesses to become successful. If it *does* take this long then it will go places and could become a million pound company – you never know. Just look at the successes of the entrepreneurs I mentioned above.

Your brand name is very important, so when you set up a company, check for a good name and ensure it's not already registered on Companies House. Lord Alan Sugar says 'Go get the business, build your clients'.

You may experience failure; some things *can* go wrong and you have to be strong. Pick yourself back up and say 'I am going to work hard and be better than ever'.

Last thing for this chapter, always stay focused on your business and be positive. Never say no? Answer is yes and it will happen.

Key points from this chapter:

- Work hard day by day,
  brick by brick.

- It's not where you start it's
  where you finish.

- Follow your mentor's success.

- Research and market your
  business well and name it wisely.

- Keep an eye on targets
  and budget well.

- Control your spending.

- Monitor your bank accounts
  weekly or monthly.

CHAPTER 8

Saving money for a rainy day

have already touched a little bit on this subject in previous chapters. As you will have learned, there are various ways of saving money. Let's start with banks and building societies.

You should set up different savings accounts for different items. Some banks charge a yearly fee of £30–£120 per year, depending on the bank, so it is important to do your research.

But how much you want to save a year in one account should be at least £120 minimum and the maximum £3000 to £5000 in the first year. For one such investment it could be purchasing a car, a new fitted kitchen or building work (if you are, of course, unable to do so yourself).

When having a saving account you should have a budget every day, week or month. You should put money in that account regularly, give it a name and keep an eye on it. Investments or funds with a high interest percentage are obviously ideal but currently the return is paltry.

If you have seven accounts and start to monitor them year-end, as an example, you could have 5k in each, which is 35k per annum. To help, you should have jars, which you can put money in every day, which we also discussed in a previous chapter. At the end of the month when you get paid, get into the good habit of taking it to the bank/building society.

Making lists of your incomings and outgoings is crucially important in order to save money, so focus on budgeting. I know I have mentioned these points many times but it is imperative. By repeating this information you will remember what you need to do and get into good habits. Only buy what you need, but also have an end of month jar for yourself to enjoy what you have earned, if you have money left over (disposable income).

If you are 'in the money' at the end of the month, it's a nice idea to call friends and family round to enjoy a meal. This way you are still in control of your cash and enjoying a great social life too.

Try to spend £10 three ways, the same with £100 or £1000. What this means is if you have £10 for your lunch per day, before going out divide it into three parts: £3 per lunch, £3 bus fare or other transport and £4 on sundries.

What this does is puts you within budget for many things. You will find more money in the bank.

Control your spending. The average person spends 30% on bills, 30% mortgage, 20% going out and 20% on saving.

You should try and save half of your earnings on savings – it might be hard but it can be achieved. If you're saving hard over ten years you should have reaped the rewards.

If you are lucky enough you may occasionally find you have overflow money (or disposable income). If you have unexpected payments to make such as a new fridge or a TV, this overflow money will help.

Saving for rainy days means that you should have money available for big expenditures such as a dream holiday, wedding or whatever it may be, or perhaps you'll want to put it straight back into the business!

That £30 you've saved by the end of the month (remember those jars?) will go towards your everyday items such as eggs, milk, bread and beans. This advice is not for every person as some people do not need to take money from their savings, but if you are in this position this is the advice I urge you to take.

If you are organised you are already halfway there. So when spending you must budget. Think before you spend. Many people do not. Money can be like gold dust.

- Unless you're very well off by now (from following my advice), try not to buy what you do not need.
- Remember the good days – even if you're

having bad days, remember that good days are just around the corner if you remember these points.

- Discipline is key.

As you can see, finding ways to save for rainy days can be quite productive. If you have read the friends and family chapter and you have a good relationship with them, they may ask to borrow money from you or you may offer it to them from time to time. You may need to borrow short-term from them and by having this great relationship, you are able to receive a loan. But if you do not have money available for rainy days you will not be able to lend it. Just be sure that if you *do* loan it out you receive it back again (hopefully with a bit of interest).

So be careful to whom you borrow the money to – making money is hard, saving it is even harder, so be wise at saving and lending. Many people will not lend you money so that is also why it is great to have good family/friend relationships.

You could also watch videos on tips for

saving money and avoiding overspending. Do not spend your hard earned money by wasting it on drinking, gambling or betting of any kind. If times are hard you must stay motivated and disciplined – you have earned that money yourself so don't go spoiling it. Also, inform your close relations if you're going through a rough patch and they may offer to help you out – that's what they're there for.

With COVID-19, things will get harder in years to come. Start investing long-term so you can build on wealth and savings. People say brick by brick you can build a house or a castle – it *is* possible. So keep saving for your growing family.

Depending on your age, it may seem a faraway prospect now but one day you will need money to purchase a mortgage or a loan for a work vehicle. If you try and follow my advice you will already have money in the bank. On-line banking is great as you have access to your funds at the touch of a few buttons and you don't need to travel to the bank every time. You can move money from different accounts too, depending on what you need them for at any one time.

Be wise and positive at all times, you will get there with the grace of God.

Key points from this chapter:

- Set up saving accounts and on-line banking.

- Budget every day/week/month.

- Don't overspend or waste your hard earned money on gambling.

CHAPTER 9

Motivation

What is motivation? It is a drive to want success. It has to be focused in your mind in order for it to help you achieve your goals. Rich people have dreams to be even richer and to have further luxuries to enjoy – why shouldn't it be you?

Having the motivation to achieve all these things is important; it is part of your physical growth that allows you to move forward towards success.

Being confident and positive are rules for pushing that motivation. Focus on your assets. Invest at all times for further growth. Many times you should be penny-wise. Remind yourself of your goals.

You must know what your target is and

where you want to be going with your life. All these factors will help motivate you. What do you wish for your family and for yourself?

Sometimes we need to make quick decisions. Focus on your plans – perfection in life is satisfying. Try and improve your lifestyle at all times. If you were planning for a nicer house you must know how many bedrooms you would like. What about the size of your garden, kitchen, garage, etc? Focus on those targets and you will find that your motivation will increase.

As mentioned earlier, day by day, brick by brick, small step by small step, work hard and you should get there earlier than you predict. If you plan targets and you reach your goal early then you know you have been successful. Even if you have a new kitchen build planned, so many people go over budget – keep to the costs, don't overspend, set the right amount in the first place and then your costs won't spiral out of control.

As this book is called *Focus on Life*, FOCUS is the key factor. If there is ever a problem, speak to your mentor, father or mother for guidance and they could help motivate and encourage you to change the situation. They may well have been through this before. Speak to them for guidance.

You will get there with the grace of God. Be positive at all times. As I've said before, find ways to make money before and after work. If I say these things many times then the message should sink in. This book is here to help you achieve your goals in the right way.

Your own success is important because your goals are to make money for further improvements in life, whatever they may be. Learn and modify your actions as you go. Always try and improve with what you are doing. Find new projects and ways to do things in the most proactive and time-appropriate way. It's also a good way of thinking.

Your emotional growth in fantasizing about being well off or rich one day is good for you. Calculate what you spend as you go along in life; sometimes it's the little costs, the sundries in life that add up more than you think.

When watching YouTube videos you will learn more skills and ways of thinking. They should motivate and inspire you in your ambition to become rich. Keep on watching and learning… or read those books I mentioned earlier. Apparently, the average person reads 3–4 books a year and business people read 50 books a year. When was the last time you read a book that inspired you? Of course, you can build this time into the time-keeping tips I provided earlier. How you motivate yourself is important.

Over time you can pass the knowledge you have learned over to your children/ grandchildren and family and friends who will agree that knowledge is power.

The best way to stay motivated is the knowledge that you *can* become successful and rich if you FOCUS on your plans. Work hard and you will get there. Hard work and perseverance will get you there in the end. Project manage your work in stages on a piece of paper. If your ideas are there on paper then you are partway to reaching your success and hopefully on track.

Also, as I said earlier, if you fail at first, try again. It may be an old cliché, but it's true. If two plans fail then one may win. Keep planning, budgeting and investing in your money and keep an eye on it through on-line banking.

Don't just look at short-term goals – look at long-term goals too. See where you want to be in ten years' time compared to where you are now with your life.

Learn from your parents and friends – tell them of your plans, update them and you will feel motivated to continue.

Remember the good days in your life, not just the bad days. Try to see all things in a positive way.

You could make lots of shorter term goals and if you achieve these you will feel you keep winning your dreams – this all helps with further motivation and then you can win the goals of your life!

The richest man in France is worth 90 billion euros and his name is Bernard Arnault. It shows what hard graft can do if you focus.

My focus is to tell people that money cannot buy happiness at all times, but it can certainly help to resolve a lot of problems; after all, every move we make in life is with money.

Unfortunately, recessions can take money away too and we have no control of it. This is why motivation is so important because it is something you can mentally control and if you have the opportunities to make money when the time is right then you should go for it.

My father saved and spent wisely. He said that when you have no money no-one wants to know you, but when you have a nice house, car or business, whatever, he said they want a piece of you. That was very sad to hear, but he has continued to motivate me throughout my life. The rich say 'Rub your shoulders with the rich and you will get richer'. Money makes money. To some extent, this is true. Please spend wisely.

Motivation is also about disciplining yourself. Get into good habits. Discipline yourself with getting up on time, getting to work on time, avoiding overspending, etc. Some people fail as there is no discipline within them and they fail on a regular basis. I hope you understand why this chapter is paramount in helping you achieve success.

Key points from this chapter:

- Try to stay positive and confident.

- Know what your target is and where you want to go.

- Ask for guidance when required.

- Complete projects proactively.

- Make short-term and long-term goals.

- Remember that you *can* achieve.

- Discipline yourself.

CHAPTER 10

Later life – retirement and an easier time

While you're working hard at 25 years of age you may fantasize about having an easier life by the age of 50 – you could semi-retire. This means that you do not *have* to work until you're 65–70 years old.

What this also means is that you should have more money in the bank as you have been able to pay your bills over the years and perhaps you have paid off your mortgage too. This frees up money to pay for your kids' weddings, parties, etc.

If you do *not* have the cash in the bank by 50 years old you may well have experienced money issues. Ideally, you will have acquired a tidy sum via investments, a pension and/or other investments or in property – perhaps around £200k, who knows? It is not millions but will lead to an easier life.

You could have had a million if you had started a business 25 years ago, for instance, and kept saving. You may have made more than a million with assets, etc. The power of money will give you, your partner and family some confidence in life. Perhaps you can now have a great car, house and business, not to mention those all-important friends, of course.

If you have read the other chapters you will remember that saving every day, week, month, no matter how small, can help you over the years. To get the gain, take the pain. Focus on working hard and it will get you there. Some people do not control money and will just withdraw £100 from their bank to go to the pub, club or restaurant and spend it.

If the same £100 was split three ways: £30 pub, £30 club, £30 restaurant, they will still have £10 in their back pocket for tomorrow, but it would be £100 if they'd kept with the budget.

If you spent the whole £100 then you need to make another trip to the bank to withdraw more money.

If you really want to retire at a reasonable age to enjoy your family, friends, good health and wealth, the rule of thumb is to spend wisely. Keep fit – do the hobbies you enjoy and you will have more time to enjoy them in later life if you have retired at a good age. Without good health you cannot enjoy good wealth. Perhaps with the good habit of getting up early you could meditate or exercise. You could be fit enough to take your grandkids to school or to the park. Perhaps they may need some new Adidas trainers? Granddad/ma could help with those (you). Going for walks or to the gym will help with keeping fit. Reading books and newspapers and doing the crossword in your lunch break will be beneficial for your mental health. When you're 65 years of age you need to make the most of your remaining life. Gardening is a great hobby in the spring and summer, so potter around in that garden or courtyard, otherwise your bones and joints could stiffen too early.

The possibilities for enjoyment in later life and/or retirement are endless. Enjoy walks in the local park after a light breakfast with orange juice and tea and with local news to listen to. You could go fishing, improve your house or finally go on your dream holiday.

Some people say retirement is boring, so plan ahead and you'll make it exciting as per all those activities mentioned above. Always have something to look forward to. People say time flies. We do not know what is around the corner, which is why it's so important to make the most of what's happening in your life now. My Dad said 'Never waste valuable time in life. Make good use of it'. Always be strong, start with a new vision and develop your self-awareness.

When you plan your life, split it into decades, which means that every ten years plan what you would like to do and how you will get there. You will reap the benefits during retirement.

Advise your grandkids what's right and wrong. Share your knowledge with them so that they too can start good money habits early in life – after all, if you have been sensible with money and health you should have more time to do this now.

When you reach 50 years of age, things should change in life. Why? Because you will not be studying or changing jobs as you did in your younger years. I started my work and education at 25 years old and had many different jobs. At 17 I had a part-time job in a Londis store, then at a cinema in central London. By the time I was 20 I was studying A levels in further studies with City & Guilds.

My first job was with the mega bookmaker William Hill and then I worked for 2–3 years as an engineer repairing TVs, cables and sound systems, etc. After that I sold hi-fis, mobile phones and accessories (that I mentioned in an earlier chapter) for about ten years, and then I moved to TV projector systems in 1999.

I began my own business in 2000 in properties. I worked my way up into investments and stock trading, etc.

Now, after 30 years or more, I look back and it seemed easy. Considering the COVID-19 pandemic we're experiencing now, all I am saying is that it was not actually that easy but hard at times.

If you have had a successful career then perhaps you're now ready to trade those walking or work boots for some slippers, IF you have remembered to set aside the monies you received from all those pay cheques – splitting the money on the day you received it – 20% to each of three savings accounts would be saving 60%. This leaves you with 40% for your bills and food. By using this method you can utilize the one account for money you need to withdraw from, which still leaves two untouched. You can continue to build on them during the course of a year.

As mentioned in previous chapters, FOCUS is always key in this game so do your budgets as much as possible. Cut out the overspending. Use those old-fashioned jars I discussed, which have been one of the longest standing ways of saving money.

Nowadays with computers, everyone is able to use spreadsheets on Excel and undertake on-line banking, which makes it easier for us to keep on track with our money. You could even put all your expenditure on there and the system will do the maths!

With a successful semi-retirement or early retirement plan, you could put your assets and pension money into an Excel spreadsheet to ensure you continue to keep track. Thirty years ago it was much harder to do this. Take the time now to acknowledge this fact and to make your life easier in years to come.

Remember, life will not come back and you are getting older every day. Take your ship to sea and make sure you know where the ship is going.

Finally, don't forget to have good manners and respect everyone. Treating people kindly, just as you would like to be treated yourself, can help bring joy to our lives!

Key points from this chapter:

- Get ready to retire – start making preparations now.

- Having a pension and money coming in at the age of 65 is paramount.

- Keep fit for your health.

- Keep your money safe.

- Make the most of now.

- Start teaching grandkids good habits.

- Respect everyone.

Conclusion

This book is about your 'life pattern', your job and how you can change it. It is also about your marriage; how you can improve your time together with loved ones and lead a more fulfilling life.

To achieve such a seemingly impossible thing, you can do various vital activities and thought processes to help this become easier, including the key points throughout this book.

Working six days a week and still having time for family and friends seems complicated, but you will find yourself in a much better position for later life.

Figure out which chores and jobs you can complete before and after work to make time for the things you wish to do, like spending time with your family.

Learn to start financial planning as soon

and as early as you can to secure your future. This planning connects to many other points discussed in this book, leaving you money for a rainy day if needed or allowing you to focus on your job first and foremost on the road to becoming successful. Even helping you become strong and independent, leading to better mental health and confidence.

If you decide to have a family of your own, motivate your children and friends to better themselves. Become their mentor and help them achieve own their goals in life.

You'll need to practice discipline to be able to reach these goals. It's a challenging aspect to nail down in one's life, but the benefits are undeniably helpful. Don't look back; focus forward. Focus on your job, your life and your family. In later life, when you're looking into retirement, you'll be secure, happy, wise and healthy.

And of course, last but most important; *focus on life—plan for a better future.*

Notes

Printed in Great Britain
by Amazon